Also by Marge Piercy

Poetry
Made in Detroit
The Hunger Moon: New & Selected Poems
The Crooked Inheritance
Colors Passing Through Us
The Art of Blessing the Day Early
Early Grrrl
Mars and Her Children
Available Light
My Mother's Body
Stone, Paper, Knife
Circles on the Water
The Moon Is Always Female
The Twelve-Spoked Wheel Flashing
Living in the Open
To Be of Use
4-Telling (*with Bob Hershon, Emmett Jarrett and Dick Lourie*)
Hard Loving
Breaking Camp

Novels
Storm Tide (*with Ira Wood*)
City of Darkness, City of Light
The Longings of Women
He, She and It
Summer People
Gone to Soldiers
Fly Away Home
Braided Lives
Vida
The High Cost of Living
Woman on the Edge of Time
Small Changes
Dance the Eagle to Sleep
Going Down Fast

Other

The Last White Class: A Play *(with Ira Wood)*
Parti--Colored Blocks for a Quilt: Essays
Early Ripening: American Women's Poetry Now: An Anthology
The Earth Shines Secretly: A Book of Days
(with paintings by Nell Blaine)

WHAT ARE

BIG GIRLS MADE OF?

Poems by Marge Piercy

 ALFRED A. KNOPF   New York 2018

THIS IS A BORZOI BOOK
PUBLISHED BY ALFRED A. KNOPF, INC.

Copyright © 1997 by Middlemarsh, Inc.

All rights reserved under International and Pan-American Copyright Conventions.
Published in the United States by Alfred A. Knopf, Inc., New York, and simulta-
neously in Canada by Random House of Canada Limited, Toronto. Distributed by
Random House, Inc., New York.

http://www.randomhouse.com/

Various poems in this collection originally appeared in the following publications:
*Ararat, Calapooya Collage, Caprice, Chiron Review, Cream City Review, DAVKA,
Free Lunch, Gutenberg, Heaven Bone, Kalliope: Women's Body Images, Kerem:
Creative Explorations in Judaism, Life on the Line: Selections on Words and
Healing, Long Shot, Lunar Calendar, The Massachusetts Review, Negative Capa-
bility, Nightsun, On the Issues, Outlet, The Plum Review, Poets On, River Styx,
Seattle Review, South Coast Poetry Journal, Southern California Anthology,
Thirteenth Moon, TIKKUN, Verve, Visions International, The Women's Review
of Books, Yellow Silk.*

Library of Congress Cataloging-in-Publication Data
Piercy, Marge.
    What are big girls made of? / by Marge Piercy.
        p.   cm.
    ISBN 0-679-45065-3 · ISBN 978-0-679-76594-3
    1. Women—Poetry.   I. Title.
  PS3566.I4W48   1997
  811'.54—dc20   96-29207
                        CIP

For Woody

and the years we go through together
in all colors of weather

Contents

THE BROTHER-LESS POEMS

Brother-less one: Sun god

In a family snapshot I stand in pigtails
grinning. I hug the two pillars
of my cracked world, my cold
father, my hot brother, the fair and the ruddy,
the grey eyed forbidder, the one who hit
but never caressed, who shouted
but never praised; and on the left, you.
You were the dark pulsating sun of my childhood,
the man whose eyes could give water
instead of ice, eyes brown as tree bark.

You were the one I looked like, as even
your children looked more like me
than like their mothers. All had the same
dark slanted Tartar eyes glinting like blades
and the same black hair rippling
coarse, abundant, grass of a tundra of night.
We are small and scrappy.
We go for the throat in anger.
We have bad genes and good minds.
We drag a load of peacock tales sweeping the dust.

Myths come into life around us
like butterflies hatching, bright and voracious.
We learned sex easily as we learned to talk

and it shaped our handshakes and our laughter.
Trouble was our shadow, tied to our heels.

Thus we grew out of the same mother
but never spoke real words since I turned twelve.
Yet you built into my psyche that space
for a man not of ice and thumbtacks,
a man who could think with his body,
a man who could laugh from the soles
of his feet, a man who could touch
skin simply as sun does.
You gave me a license
for the right of the body to joy.

Brother-less two: Palimpsest

My friend Elizabeth said, the week you died
and your widow would not have me at
your funeral, you and your brother:
both had great wild imaginations.
You put yours into books.
He rewrote himself.

I can remember the last honest talking that ever
went between us, strong, jolting to me
as straight bourbon to a child not used to beer.

You were just back from the war,
still a Marine, crazy on experimental
drugs for malaria, and you poured
the whole Pacific war into my ears
till I was raw and blistered.
Forty years later I could hear your voice,
I could see the women falling into the sea,
I could see the rotting bodies on the coral.
I remember your talking of the smell of battle,
of shit when bodies break open,
how blood stinks like spoiled meat.

You talked about how you had been promoted
then busted for hitting your sergeant,
time in stockade, beaten for being

a Jew, for being short, for having
a temper like a piñata breaking.

You were back to divorce Florence,
your second wife. You brought souvenirs
of the occupation, silks, a kimono,
glass animals, little saki cups, photos
of you with buddies, geishas, captured flags.
You marched on and on as the medicine burned
in you. I was the pit into which you shoveled
memories and then walked off.

You winked at me and you began to whistle.
In your mind you began to change the sky,
the water, the land. The stories turned
from yellow to blue. The blood turned
to paint. It smelled like glory.
It was the Fourth of July all year
and the war became a recruiting poster
featuring you.

Brother-less three: Never good enough

Susie was my niece; she was not
your daughter: you refused her
the way someone will send back the wrong
dish in a restaurant.
The way you turned from the sons
of your third marriage. In a pique
you had a vasectomy, saying that no child
of yours ever did it right.

Did what? You seemed to have no love
to spare for them, as you pretended
your first three wives were one
dead woman. For twelve years
we had only an occasional card.

What is a half brother? Half time?
Half there? Half brother and half not?
We had different fathers. The
year before your bar mitzvah, our mother
eloped with my father. Your father
took out her desertion on you.

When you were sixteen, my parents
caught you fucking your girlfriend Isabel,

forced you to marry. They tried
that on me at eighteen. I yelled
I'd take off and she'd never see me again.
A pit lined with fur and barbed wire;
roast chicken and plastique, warmth
and bile, a kiss and a razor in the ribs,
our family.

These memories tangle, a fine gold chain
with invisible barbs. As I pick out knots,
always there are tighter knots inside,
my fingers bleed
and a poison works in me
boiling up fever.

I see you thirteen with your father beating
you on the back and shoulders, screaming
at our mother the whore. I see you fifteen
when my father decided to adopt you,
a runaway eating garbage in alleys,
looking for someplace you felt at home.
Later I would hitchhike over half the globe
looking for that secret warm place
we once made briefly for each other.

We both felt the world as a great pain
in the middle of our being, and we each
set out to change it: our separate ways.

I remember coming to see you in L.A. in '64.
I was in civil rights. Black friends
told me L.A. was bad, stewing, smell of raw
sewage on smoggy mornings, hope eviscerated.
You said, We have no Negroes here.

Each link, a barb. Each set of links,
a knot I could never pick free.
My palms are crisscrossed with scars
as from barbed wire.

By then you were a college graduate—
who had not finished high school.
By then, your father was a Frenchman,
a French Catholic. By then, you were
a Marine hero with medals and war stories
you shared at the VFW. You drank martinis
instead of boilermakers. You speculated
in real estate near that huge
stinking sink the Salton Sea

where drowned rats wash up by the flooded
motels and the desert is laid out
with sidewalks and street signs.

Once when I read poetry in your city
you came. Afterwards you stared at me.
Why do you remember those old sad things?
Why do these people come to hear you?
That old stuff, who cares?
Ah, but you cared. You could not look
me in the eyes. You could not risk
one real word
for fear I would like a big bad wolf
blow your house down
with my voice of fire.

Brother-less four: Liars' dance

The myth says, he left three women,
three children, his family; his best friend
he left to die alone, so he was lonely
and unloved to the bitter end.

We live far more in fractals than in grids.
His fourth wife was a Chicana, a widow
with four children who had a house
in a good section of the L.A. hills.
Of all his wives and girlfriends,
she alone resembled our mother—
small, dark, busty, flirtatious
she smiled easily and lied,
as well as he did, but not to him.

She was Spanish, an old colonial
family; he was French.
They were passionate to be proper.
Their house was papered with genealogies,
an aristocracy of Oz, detailed
as the papers of a prize schnauzer,
a past elaborated, documented
with the zeal of federal marshals
protecting a star witness.

Maybe I should simply see it
as a mating dance, two cranes
stepping about each other transfixed,

the ritual of two hot lovers
in bed pretending to be children
or Klingons or dogs—extending
the role for thirty years.
Like lovebirds in a cage,
they did not tire of the mirror
or each other.

Brother-less five: Truth as a cloud of moths

In adolescence I tried on others'
styles, shrugged on a leather coat
of tough street kid I had thrown off
to run the college marathon;
turned existentialist in black
turtleneck and black jeans;
played vamp, played Romeo
and Juliet alternate nights,
played dissolute writer, mama
bear, pal and litterateur.

I would copy bits from movies,
wriggle my hips like this one,
pout like that. I thrust myself
into dramas and slithered out.

I've always seen the alternate
lives, the faces I might have worn
had I left the party with this man
or that instead of going alone
into the night's soft rumble;
had I paused when the golden balls
were thrown before me on the race
course like Atalanta, instead
of laughing coarsely and running on.

Had I been a little more courageous
or a little less; less curious

to taste whatever brew was handed
me; had I not picked up and gone,
letting the door slam, then I would
see and not see through different eyes.

Variant selves haunt
the corridors of my brain, people
my novels, crowd in like ghosts
drawn to blood when friends
or strangers tell me secrets,
hand me their troubles,
sweaters knit of hair and wire.

Why then have I stalked for years
round and round the self you
built of forged documents,
stories lifted from magazines,
charm, sweat and subterfuge
as if I were the sentinel of truth?
Maybe we just like the taste
of different lies.

Brother-less six: Unconversation

I buzz irritating and persistent
darting, biting at your death.
What do I hope to understand?
Why do I grieve for someone I did not know?

I was a white cedar swamp you traversed
on a wooden walkway above the black water.
You were a closet from which odd toys
and bizarre tools fell out on my head.

Our conversations were conducted
without a common language.
I gave you a foot. You handed me a balloon.
You gave me spurs. I passed you marmalade.

You looked at my books
as if they were soiled panties
I had left in the livingroom.
You would not touch them.

Always I entertained fantasies
like friends who used to be close

about my father and about you:
that someday we would truly talk.

I wanted to parley between the forts.
You thought I bore the past
like a broad sword swinging
to cleave you from your fictions,

and perhaps you were right
to defend yourself. I am impolite
as wind that blows umbrellas wrong
side to and dead leaves down.

I cannot stay out of crevices.
I cannot abstain from tipping
things over and stirring up dust.
You closed doors and windows against me

and stayed safe. I make you up now
out of pain you deposited in me decades

ago, eggs of blood red dragonflies.
Your abandoned history became me.

I put out stories like weird fruit,
a cheap mail order novelty: GROW PEACHES
PLUMS, KIWIS, APPLES ON THE SAME TREE.
Grandma's tales, mother's, your history,

the sagas of friends and strangers:
you are stirred and mixed with them
in the incandescent melting pot of my mind.
I mother you into new ferment

who would not brother me.

Brother-less seven: Endless end

I have trouble understanding
when something is done
that was not finished.

I have to let you go
since I lack a hold,
no connection beyond a history

you had abandoned
like worn out clothes
delivered to Goodwill.

Lives are full of broken dishes
and promises, stories left
half told, apologies

that come back like letters
with insufficient postage,
keys that open no known doors.

The abandoned live with an absence
that shaped them like the canyon
of a river gone dry.

Do I mourn you, Phoenix hedonist,
or the man in the mirror
you killed in 1945,

because he was dragging you down?
I have made my own brothers,
my sisters. It is hard

to say goodbye to nothing
personal, mouthfuls bitten off
of silence and wet ashes.

WHAT ARE BIG GIRLS MADE OF?

What are big girls made of?

The construction of a woman:
a woman is not made of flesh
of bone and sinew
belly and breasts, elbows and liver and toe.
She is manufactured like a sports sedan.
She is retooled, refitted and redesigned
every decade.

Cecile had been seduction itself in college.
She wriggled through bars like a satin eel,
her hips and ass promising, her mouth pursed
in the dark red lipstick of desire.

She visited in '68 still wearing skirts
tight to the knees, dark red lipstick,
while I danced through Manhattan in mini skirt,
lipstick pale as apricot milk,
hair loose as a horse's mane. Oh dear,
I thought in my superiority of the moment,
whatever has happened to poor Cecile?
She was out of fashion, out of the game,
disqualified, disdained, dis-
membered from the club of desire.

Look at pictures in French fashion
magazines of the 18th century:
century of the ultimate lady

fantasy wrought of silk and corseting.
Paniers bring her hips out three feet
each way, while the waist is pinched
and the belly flattened under wood.
The breasts are stuffed up and out
offered like apples in a bowl.
The tiny foot is encased in a slipper
never meant for walking.
On top is a grandiose headache:
hair like a museum piece, daily
ornamented with ribbons, vases,
grottoes, mountains, frigates in full
sail, balloons, baboons, the fancy
of a hairdresser turned loose.
The hats were rococo wedding cakes
that would dim the Las Vegas strip.
Here is a woman forced into shape
rigid exoskeleton torturing flesh:
a woman made of pain.

How superior we are now: see the modern woman
thin as a blade of scissors.
She runs on a treadmill every morning,
fits herself into machines of weights
and pulleys to heave and grunt,
an image in her mind she can never
approximate, a body of rosy

glass that never wrinkles,
never grows, never fades. She
sits at the table closing her eyes to food
hungry, always hungry:
a woman made of pain.

A cat or dog approaches another,
they sniff noses. They sniff asses.
They bristle or lick. They fall
in love as often as we do,
as passionately. But they fall
in love or lust with furry flesh,
not hoop skirts or push up bras
rib removal or liposuction.
It is not for male or female dogs
that poodles are clipped
to topiary hedges.

If only we could like each other raw.
If only we could love ourselves
like healthy babies burbling in our arms.
If only we were not programmed and reprogrammed
to need what is sold us.
Why should we want to live inside ads?
Why should we want to scourge our softness
to straight lines like a Mondrian painting?
Why should we punish each other with scorn

as if to have a large ass
were worse than being greedy or mean?

When will women not be compelled
to view their bodies as science projects,
gardens to be weeded,
dogs to be trained?
When will a woman cease
to be made of pain?

Pop-sicle

Martina had a mama, Anna-Lisa
and a papa and a house on the corner
of the block with a birch tree
and Herbie the Hamster.
Herbie let her carry him in her blouse
and never bit her, although
his claws were pins sticking her.

When her papa yelled, Herbie would
wake too and scrabble in his cage.
His beady eyes looked at her without
a moment's anger and never swelled
with tears like her mama's.
Papa would pull on her and
then Mama would pull on her.

Then Mama took her to Grandma.
A week after they moved into
Mama's old room, Herbie died.
Mama put him in a box
in the freezer till the ground thawed.
Mama got a job in a doctor's office.
They moved to a yellow brick building.

Anna-Lisa got sick and lost the job.
They lived with Mama's boyfriend

Carl and then back to sour Grandma
and then to new boyfriend Jerry.
Herbie goes along in his box.
Spring has come and gone and come
and gone four times, but Martina

will not give Herbie to the embrace
of somebody else's earth. He is
her lost love, her cropped roots
as they move from one man's apartment
to another man's house. They are not
fathers. Martina glares at the men from
slitted eyes. Herbie's still frozen.

Elegy in rock, for Audre Lorde

A child, I cherished a polyhedron of salt
my father brought up from under Detroit,
the pure crystal from a deep mine.
The miracle was it felt hard and clear
as glass and yet the tongue said tears.

My other treasure was a polished shard
of anthracite that glittered on my palm,
harder, fiercer than the soft coal
we shoveled into the basement furnace.
Coal halfway to a diamond?

More than once we talked about rocks
for which you had a passion, curiosity
fired by adventure, reading the landscape
with eye and pick, cliffs that confided
in a lover's whisper their history.

Obsidian, the obvious: it can take
an edge, can serve as a knife
in ritual or in combat, as your fine
dark deep voice could pour out love,
could take an edge like a machete.

Carnelian lips, black and rose marble
metamorphosed rock blasted into beauty:
but what you are now that only the work

remains is garnet, not a flashy
jewel, native, smouldering, female.

Garnet: the blackest red,
color of the inner woman, of deep sex,
color of the inside of the lid closed tight
while the eye still searches
for light in itself.

Sand is the residue,
the pulverized bones of mountains.
Here on the great beach in summer
the sea rolls over and bares
slabs of tawny sand that glitter:

little buffed worlds of garnet
pool like the shadows of old blood
under the sun's yellow stare.
On my palm they wink, this shading
like rouge stippling the sand.

You told me of a garnet big as a child's
head, you told me of garnet glowing
like women's stories pulled from the dust,

garnets you freed into the sun,
lying on your palm like summer nights.

Rich darkness I praise, dark richness,
the true color of a live pulsing heart,
blackberries in strong sunlight,
crow's colors, black tulip chalices,
the city sky glowering from the plain.

Audre, Audre, your work shines on the night
of the world, the blaze of your words,
but your own female power and beauty
are gone, a garnet ground into powder
and dissolved in wine the earth drinks.

A day in the life

She is wakened at four a.m.
Of course she does not
pick up, but listens
through the answering machine
to the male voice promising
she will burn in hell.

At seven she opens her door.
A dead cat is hammered
to her porch: brown tabby.
Hit by a car, no collar.
She hugs her own Duke of Orange.
She cannot let him out.

She has her car locked
in a neighbor's garage,
safe from pipe bombs, but
she must walk there. She drives
to work by a circuitous route.
Never the same way twice.

Outside the clinic three
men walk in circles with photos
of six-month fetuses.
They surround her car.
They are forbidden the parking
lot but police don't care.

They bang on her hood.
As she gets out, they bump

and jostle her. One thrusts
his sign into her face.
She protects her eyes.
Something hard strikes her back.

Inside she sighs. Turns on
the lights, the air
conditioning, the coffee
machine. The security system
is always on. The funds
for teenage contraception,

gone into metal detectors.
She answers the phone.
"Is this where you kill babies?"
The second call a woman
is weeping. The day begins.
A girl raped by her stepfather,

a harried mother with too
many children and diabetes,
a terrified teenager who does
not remember how it happened,
a woman with an injunction
against an abuser. All day

she takes their calls,
all day she checks them in,
takes medical histories,
holds hands, dries tears,

hears secrets and lies and
horrors, soothes, continues.

Every time a new patient
walks in, a tinny voice
whispers, is this the one
carrying a handgun, with
an automatic weapon, with
a knife? She sits exposed.

She answers the phone.
"I'm going to cut your throat,
you murderer." "Have
a nice day." A bomb threat
is called in. She has
to empty the clinic.

The police finally come.
There is no bomb. The
doctor tells her how they
are stalking his daughter.
Then she goes home to Duke.
Eats a late supper by the TV.

Her mother calls. Her
boyfriend comes over. She
cries in his arms. He is,

she can tell, getting tired
of her tears. Next morning
she rises and day falls

on her like a truckload
of wet cement. This is
a true story, this is
what I know of virtue,
this is what I know
of goodness in our time.

The promotion

My friend has become an administrator.
First they welded his clothes
to his newly rigid body
so he would never   even
in the shower   stand naked.

Then he went on a pompous fast,
nothing but stuffed derma,
hot air and those little plastic
worms used for packing, defatted
lunch meats, white bread.

His brain was scraped, then
shellacked against mildew; thermostat
turned down for efficiency,
adrenals replaced by reaction
meters, poll results flashed

every minute on his retina.
Alert to every fluctuation
in the atmosphere of opinion,
ready to jettison ideas
at the first turbulence,

he is prepared to take the helm
and steer the course of the giant
hot air balloon of destiny,
taking an oath he will
never deflate or look down.

A little monument

One unknown martyr of civil rights
was my love at age fourteen,
an altered male tabby of serene disposition,
a furry Buddha, last of my string
of childhood cats named by my mother:
Whiskers, Buttons, Fluffy.

He came in from the alley one sodden morning
bony under mats of clotted fur.
In a week he doubled his girth.
He would eat anything with pleasure,
catfood, human, oatmeal, cantaloupe.
He washed his face and paws after, purring.

Trustingly he sprawled on his back, belly up
on my father's workbench, the refrigerator,
under a chair, in the window watching the street.
He was lord of the little back yard and the porch.
When the neighbor's yellow dog barked,
he crouched and blinked. Soon he was sitting

on the fence just out of reach, smiling.
He slept on the foot of my bed every night;
in winter he crawled under the covers.
My parents were selling the tiny house,

an asbestos shack, but no one would buy
except Blacks. The neighborhood was changing,

everybody said, and run down. We sold
to a Black doctor. Next day we were moving,
and my old boyfriend next door poisoned
my cat. He was always grateful for food,
he always washed his face and purred afterward.
It took him all night to die.

My head was a jumble of prejudices repeated
and Black girls and boys real as my hands,
but it was my cat who recruited me
for civil rights years later in Ann Arbor,
Chicago, a gentle cat with a stupid name
who sent me marching and shouting for justice.

Half vulture, half eagle

I saw it last night, the mortgage
bird with heavy hunched shoulders
nesting in shredded hundred dollar bills
its long curved claws seize, devour.

You feed it and feed it in hopes
it will grow smaller. Does this make
sense? After five years of writing
checks on the first day of every month

it is swollen and red eyed and hungry.
It has passed from owner to owner,
sold by the bank to Ohio and thence
to an ersatz company that buys up slave

mortgages and is accountable to Panama
or perhaps Luxembourg, cannot be
communicated with by less than four lawyers
connected end to end like Christmas

tree light sets and blinking in six
colors simultaneously by fax.
It says, I squat on the foot of your
bed when the medical bills shovel in.

When your income withers like corn
stalks in a Kansas drought, I laugh

with a sound of sand hitting a windshield,
laughter dry as parched kernels from which

all water has been stolen by the sun.
Each month I wring you a little more.
I own a corner of your house, say
the northeast corner the storms hit

when they roar from the blast of the sea
churned into grey sudsy cliffs, and as
the storm bashes the dunes into sand
it washes away, so I can carry off

your house any time you fail to feed
me promptly. Your misfortune is my
best gamble. I am the mortgage bird
and my weight is on your back.

The grey flannel sexual harassment suit

The woman in the sexual harassment
suit should be a virgin
who attended church every Sunday,
only ten thousand miles on her
back and forth to the pew.
Her immaculate house is
bleached with chlorine tears.

The woman in the sexual harassment
suit should never have known
a man other than her father
who kissed her only
on the cheek, and the minister
who patted her head
with his gloves on.

The woman in the sexual harassment
suit is visited by female
angels only, has a platinum
hymen protected by Brinks,
is white of course as unpainted
plaster, naturally blonde
and speaks only English.

The woman in the sexual harassment
suit wears white cotton blouses

buttoned to the throat, small
pearl clip-on earrings,
grey or blue suits and one
inch heels with nylons.
Her nails and lips are pink.

If you are other than we have
described above, please do
not bother to complain.
You are not a lady.
We cannot help you.
A woman like you simply
cannot be harassed.

All systems are up

You dial and a voice answers.
After you have stammered a reply
into dead air, you realize
it cannot hear or know you.
The pre-programmed voice of a thing
addresses you as a retarded dog:

Press 0 if you wish to be connected
to emergency services. Press 1
to order a product. Press 2
to speak to an agent. Press 3
if you need assistance.
Have a nice day.

I press 3. I need information.
Another robot says, Press 1
if you wish to order a product.
Press 2 to speak to an agent
—who bleeds? Press 3 if
you need further assistance.

I press 3. The voice says,
You have pressed 3.
That is not a valid number.
Please press 4 and make

another choice. I press 4.
The canned voice speaks:

Press 3 if you desire euthanasia.
Press 2 if you wish to detonate.
Press 1 never to have been born.
Press 0 if you intend
universal Armageddon.
Have a nice day.

Between two Hamlets

He married me for reasons of state.
Said I was too fleshy the first night.
He liked girls, slender, barely fledged,
simpering, giggling in his bed.
I could hear through the wall:
the sobbing, the sharp crack of his
palm, his fist against small flesh.

Once we had our son, he was done with
me. After the endless greasy courses,
the toasts, the trumpets baying,
the flattery reeking like cheap perfume,
the whispering in corners after me,
the cold wind to sleep with,
grey pits of splintered dream.

I spoiled my son from the beginning.
Who else had I to love but lap dogs,
Ophelia who recalled my battered innocence
and the son of my pain and bed of ice
and iron, my son whom I tried to enclose
in the large warm rose of my love,
who had his father's name but not his nature.

I never told him Laertes was his own
brother, for of course the King had had
Polonius's much too young wife before
the old man bedded her. When she passed

twenty she was too old for him, dead
meat he said. Women smelled. Only
the green flesh of girls was clean.

How could two brothers have been
more different than the King,
the elder iron Hamlet, and Claudius?
The first time he touched my breast,
my heart melted like sweet butter
on a flame. The first time his hands
moved over my body, I loved him.

Passion caught me up like a leaf
and bore me on its hot wind, and my
body danced in that wind and grew
ripe at last. Yes, we killed him,
the only way we could be together,
loving as my husband never loved,
he who had broken so many girls.

We killed him and I wept and forgot him.
He was like a bad winter past, and I
could vaguely remember I had been cold,
my limbs numb as the stones of the castle.
Then my son like a sword plunged

into my new marriage to sunder my life.
He dissolved me in shame's acid.

Thus we all ended up dead, piled
like stones to make a cairn for that
King loved by nobody but his son.
I wondered often those raddled days,
did Hamlet love that nasty ghost
or did his desperate guilt walk about
the night wearing the King's busy sword?

All day all night talk radio

The voice roars from the radio
like a freight from a tunnel
and every car carries the same
coke load of fury.

The molten steel pours into
the listening ear, and there
in the snoozing brain
it ignites and sears.

How familiar it feels, this anger
that says, they took it from
you, the stuff you almost had,
the thing you wanted

to which you and only you
and those like you are entitled.
You had a deed to the castle.
You owned the sun.

Now those others are demanding
your dream stuff, red ants
biting your ass like cayenne.
If others take pieces

what's left you besides this
spite you chew like gristle

left from a bad greasy hamburger
stuck in your teeth.

If you want to shoot anyone
how about the rabid dog of your anger
howling all night at the benign
public moon?

The thief

Dina sent me a postcard,
history at a glance,
Sonka of the golden hand,
the notorious thief
being put in chains.

She looks young still, dark hair,
unsmiling—why would she?
1915, surrounded by Russian men
two blacksmiths preparing
the chains and three soldiers
to guard her, weaponless.

A Jew from Odessa, she could
move faster than water
as quiet as a leaf growing
more lightly than a shaft
of sun tapping your arm.

Like all young women
she was full of desires
little hot pomegranate seeds
bursting in her womb,
wishes crying from the dull
mirror of poverty.

Sonka heard the voices calling
from inside the coins,

take me, Sonka, take me
turn me into something sweet
turn me into something warm and soft
a cashmere shawl, a silk mantilla
a coat of fur like a bed of loving.

Eat me, said the chicken.
Drink me, the brandy sang.
Wear me, the blouse whispered.

Sonka of the golden hands
stands in the grim yard
of the prison, with her quick
hands bound in iron bracelets
calling with her solemn eyes

let me go, oh you who stare
at me and jail me in your
camera, now at last
free me to dance again
as I freed
those captured coins.

The new Rock Island Line

The Rock Island Line is the road to ride,
Leadbelly sang, a hub of railroads,
industrial city flanked by two rivers,
Rock easing into the Mississippi
just past the arsenal island
where Confederate soldiers were penned.

Empty streets. An old car in the distance
at four p.m. driven by a wizened man—
only the Miller Lite cap showing in the wind
shield beneath two fuzzy green dice—
smoking faster than he drives.

The downtown suggests alien abduction.
The buildings are intact but not even
the yellow dog of a spaghetti western
trots down the street at noon.
The used furniture store is locked
and you must ring for five minutes
before a suspicious aging hippy
will let you in to view chipped
Formica tables and tilting bridge lamps.
Yet there are twenty bars crowding
the sidewalk like pigs at a trough:
GIRLS LIVE GIRLS COUNTRY MUSIC LIVE.

Then the tourist busses arrive and park
end to end like processional caterpillars

marching not to despoil but be despoiled.
After five the parking lots fill quickly
like a shift change coming on. Down
on the levee the gambling boats are docked.
Couples in exercise gear with fanny
packs and old men on walkers, guys from
pickups jostle at a hot clip into the casinos.

Once they made farm machinery here.
Once they ran a railroad. They made
rubbers and galoshes. Now they wait smiling
dressed up in costumes out of B musicals
for tourists to give them compulsive money.

I grew up in Detroit. I can't romanticize
assembly line work; and I knew railroad firemen
and gandy dancers, the Brotherhood men,
hard work, long hours and danger.
Still they were doing something useful,
a product, a real train hooting
a promise of attainable distance.

Now the only job in town is diddling
tourists. The new Rock Island line goes,
there's a sucker getting off the bus
every minute. This town like a catfish
feeds on the bottom mud.

For two women shot to death in Brookline, Massachusetts

How dare a woman choose?
Choose to be pregnant
choose to be childless
choose to be lesbian
choose to have two lovers or none
choose to abort
choose to live alone
choose to walk alone
at night
choose to come and to go
without permission
without leave
without a man.

Consider a woman's blood
spilled on a desk,
pooled on an office floor,
an ordinary morning at work,
an ordinary morning of helping
other women choose
to be or not to be
pregnant.

A woman young and smiling
sitting at a desk
trying to put other women at ease
now bleeds from five
large wounds, bleeding

from her organs
bleeding out her life.

A young man is angry at women
women who say no
women who say maybe and mean no
women who won't
women who do and they shouldn't.
If they are pregnant they are bad
because that proves
they did it with someone,
they did it
and should die.

A man gets angry with a woman
who decides to leave him
who decides to walk off
who decides to walk
who decides.

Women are not real to such men.
They should behave as meat.
Such men drag them into the woods
and stab them
climb in their windows and rape them
such men shoot them in kitchens
such men strangle them in bed
such men lie in wait

and ambush them in parking lots
such men walk into a clinic
and kill the first woman they see.

In harm's way:
meaning in the way of a man
who is tasting his anger
like rare steak.
A daily ordinary courage
doing what has to be done
every morning, every afternoon
doing it over and over
because it is needed
put them in harm's way.

Two women dying
because a man chose that they die.
Two women dying
because they did their job
helping other women survive.
Two women dead
from the stupidity of an ex altar boy
who saw himself
as a fetus
who pumped his sullen fury
automatically
into the woman in front of him
twice, and intended more.

Stand up now and say No More.
Stand up now and say We will not

be ruled by crazies and killers,
by shotguns and bombs and acid.
We will not dwell in the caves of fear.
We will make each other strong.
We will make each other safe.
There is no other monument.

SALT IN THE AFTERNOON

Moonburn

I stayed under the moon too long.
I am silvered with lust.

Dreams flick like minnows through my eyes.
My voice is trees tossing in the wind.

I loose myself like a flock of blackbirds
storming into your face.

My lightest touch leaves blue prints,
bruises on your mind.

Desire sandpapers your skin
so thin I read the veins and arteries

maps of routes I will travel
till I lodge in your spine.

The night is our fur.
We curl inside it licking.

Liars' dice

The lies march out bravely
between us to be exchanged,
one for the other, spies
traded at the neutral border.

Our memories are wrestlers,
each trying to pin the other,
for to touch earth
or fact admits defeat.

Some lies are defensive,
I didn't do it, I
wouldn't touch the stuff,
I've never seen her before.

Others seek to scald,
burrow their way inward,
prick, draw blood, flee.
But we lie for distance,

setting between us these
fragile busy constructs
all wire, papier mache,
little dancing robots

tutus and flashing lights
wrought with far more effort
and art than we bothered
to put into love.

A warm place becomes a cold place

1

A black hole
where there used to be shining.
Energy is sucked there
transformed into spite.

This is a hunger
that can never be stuffed
into peace, for whatever
it grabs, at once alters.

Things change into their
opposites, the pressure
flattens all curves,
colors fade into darkness.

Everything boils down
to a point, then goes
into nothingness in your
eyes of ice.

2

You are traveling from me
like a bullet shot straight up

that will return aimlessly
but never harmlessly

to earth. Your anger
is an engine that has consumed
your past, is stoked now
by the present as you break

it into kindling, grind
it into sawdust. Now
you burn down the future
to speed and soot.

3

This star has died.
The last light has ridden
through cold eternity.

Somewhere in a far galaxy
perhaps its red-shifted
aura still pretends

to a life burned out
slowly, slowly and then
an explosion of fury.

Now you are a pit where
kindness, joy, the gentle
impulses fall and fail;

where light is squeezed
to darkness, where now
means only absence.

All lovers have secret names

The day I forget to write
the day I forget to feed the cats
the day I forget to love you
the day I forget your name
and then my own.

Until then I will not cease
this spinning pattern: part weave
of skeins of soft wool to keep
us warm, to clothe our too open
flesh, to decorate us—

and part dance, through woods
where roots trip me, a dance
through meadows of rabbit holes
and old ribs of plowing hidden
under thick grass.

Until then I will whirl
through my ragged days.
Like a spindle, like a dreydl
I will turn in the center
of my intricate weave

spelling your name in my dance
in my weaving, in my work,
your hidden name which
is simply, finally,
love.

Little acts of love

Shaking out clean sheets
that crisp lightly scented caress,
I make my bed ready for you.

I wash my hair, trim
nails lest they scratch you—
unintentionally.

A new paisley cloth on it,
I sit at the table
studying recipes.

Each recipe is a dance
of seduction, beckoning.
Soon the door will swing wide

to where I wait in my body
crowned and glittering
for the feast to start.

The negative ion dance

The ocean reopens us.
The brass doors in the forehead swing wide.
Light enters us like a swarm of bees
and bees turn into white petals falling.

The lungs expand as the salt air
stretches them, and they sing, treble
bagpipes eerie and serpentine.
The bones lighten to balsa wood.

The head bobs on air currents
like a bright blue balloon without ballast.
The arms want to flap. The terns
dive around us giving hopeless instruction.

Light is sharp, serrated, a flight of saws.
Light enters us and is absorbed like water,
like radiation. We take the light in
and darken it. We look just the same.

We shine only in the back of the eyes
if you stare into them as you kiss.
The light leaks out through the palms
as they caress you later in the dark.

Dance of the trees

Little sister, little sister,
you weep green tears:
the small leaves of aspens.

Little sister, be welcome in their house.
The wife will feed you soup
and lend you shawls and pillows.

Little sister, your wound
opens and closes, opens
and closes like a mouth full of teeth.

Now you are weeping in her arms.
Now she is off at work and you smile
at her husband and your breasts shimmer.

Didn't you suspect something? I asked.
Never, the wife said, *for her pain
blinded me like sun in a mirror.*

*Now little sister is comforted and huge.
Now I am the one alone.
Now I am the willow tree.*

Your standard mid life crisis

A friend is destroying his life
like a set of dishes
he has tired of, is breaking
for the noise.

The old wife is older
of course. She promises
nothing but what he knows
he can have.

She is an oak rocking chair,
sturdy, plain, shapely,
something he has taken comfort
in for years.

This one flirts like a firefly,
on and off, on and off.
Where will she flash next?
In his pocket.

She mirrors his needs,
she sends him messages to decode
twisted in his hair, knotted
in his skin.

With me you will forget failure.
With me you will be another.

My youth will shave your years
to smooth fresh skin.

He careens downhill, throwing off
books, children, history,
tossing friends, pledges, knowledge
down into the crystal canyon.

There every cliff reflects her
face with the eyes illuminating
him like a votive candle, doomed
to drip itself out.

Duet that trails off

I don't guess well, I say,
I read the Tarot, not minds.
Talk to me as if you meant
to tell the truth. What do you want?

The trail of crumbs is carefully
laid down by an adult in child
mask who knows every morsel
will vanish in an hour.

Find me, find me not.
Guess what I am wanting
here in the thicket of briars
that catch in your hair.

How can I find a single hair
in a field? How can I
trace the footsteps of someone
who will not touch ground?

If you loved me, you would
catch me. If you loved me,
you would be with me
here where I have locked myself

inside the iron fortress
within the glass mountain

on the island of falling rocks
in the sea of frivolous storms.

The birds have eaten the crumbs.
The iron has rusted like old blood.
The glass mountain is opaque with age.
The key lies on the bottom of the sea.

Salt in the afternoon

The room is a conch shell
and echoing in it, the blood
rushes in the ears,
the surf of desire sliding in
on the warm beach.

The room is the shell of the moon
snail, gorgeous predator
whose shell winds round and round
the color of moonshine
on your pumping back.

The bed is a slipper shell
on which we rock, opaline
and pearled with light sweat,
two great deep currents
colliding into white water.

The clam shell opens.
The oyster is eaten.
The squid shoots its white ink.
Now there is nothing but warm
salt puddles on the flats.

Belly good

A heap of wheat, says the Song of Songs
but I've never seen wheat in a pile.
Apples, potatoes, cabbages, carrots
make lumpy stacks, but you are sleek
as a seal hauled out in the winter sun.

I can see you as a great goose egg
or a single juicy and fully ripe peach.
You swell like a natural grassy hill.
You are symmetrical as a Hopewell mound,
with the eye of the navel wide open,

the eye of my apple, the pear's port
window. You're not supposed to exist
at all this decade. You're to be flat
as a kitchen table, so children with
roller skates can speed over you

like those sidewalks of my childhood
that each gave a different roar under
my wheels. You're required to show
muscle striations like the ocean
sand at ebb tide, but brick hard.

Clothing is not designed for women
of whose warm and flagrant bodies
you are a swelling part. Yet I confess

I meditate with my hands folded on you,
a maternal cushion radiating comfort.

Even when I have been at my thinnest,
you have never abandoned me but curled
round as a sleeping cat under my skirt.
When I spread out, so do you. You like
to eat, drink and bang on another belly.

In anxiety I clutch you with nervous fingers
as if you were a purse full of calm.
In my grandmother standing in the fierce sun
I see your cauldron that held eleven children
shaped under the tent of her summer dress.

I see you in my mother at thirty
in her flapper gear, skinny legs
and then you knocking on the tight dress.
We hand you down like a prize feather quilt.
You are our female shame and sunburst strength.

The puzzle

1

We were like pieces of a jigsaw puzzle
going about trying to find where we fit
snugly, forcing ourselves, bashing
our sharp corners flat trying to work
ourselves into angles we never suited.

Tab A into Slot B, in theory
simple enough. We hear spring peepers
going at it in puddle orgies.
The praying mantis snacking on the head
of her mate does not linger

to debate if he is Mr. Right.
Yet we fit clumsily, demand
excisions, deletions, ask for
less flesh and more credit.
Is there a larger picture we inhabit?

2

When two bodies slide together
and begin to crawl into each other's
belly and mind, how often the hard

hips bang like broken shutters,
the head goes rolling under the bed.

3

Broken marriages are carted to the junkyard,
fenders scarred from old collisions,
bodies rusted till they crumble like brick
dust, motors stripped and smoking,
what can be salvaged already stolen.

4

That we found each other in the market
of bad dreams where old clothes
flap in the north wind of despair
and tried each other on and had
the courage to clutch hard, hold on

is the unbroken stone of miracle
hidden in the center of our lives.
This magnetic core lets us walk over
our little earth and not fall off
as we turn through savage seasons.

The retreat

Come back to me.
Crawl from the cotton batting
tunnels of your obsessions,
the involuted maze without a center,
an entrance but no exit
except all at once.
If you but shut your eyes and rise
you would sail out
like a red balloon.

You are a jeweled spider
spinning an embroidered web
but it is not to catch prey:
it surrounds you.
You stalk and trap yourself.
As hunger wizens you
you spin faster and faster
until the web
darkens your world.

You stumble across a field
in a mist so thick
it chokes you. The fog
moves with you. It is only

six feet thick.
Come out to me, come out.
There are no miracles here.
Only light, sky, soil, air,
a woman with arms open.

These ravens feasting
on your wounds, they are your pets.
You called them from the cliffs
where the broken fortresses
of old defeats look picturesque.
Worry is work like any other
but no product except itself.
Come back. Let the simple light
enter and scrub your mind.

Reshaping each other

We are differently shaped
with everyone we love,
sticking out here, receding
there, interlocking couples.

We grow roles as trees
extrude bark; perhaps
the real life is under
neath in the thin green sap.

I am the finder of things
in drawers; I make lists
and menus; I read maps.
You lift and haul and open.

I select; you reject.
You brood and I fuss.
You dream and I arrange.
You regret and I flee.

If we are yin and yang
it is in a crazy quilt
of push, pull and merge.
Strange as sphinxes,

common as goldfish, neither
alike nor different finally
but ratcheted together
in the gears of marriage.

On guard

I want you for my bodyguard,
to curl round each other like two socks
matched and balled in a drawer.

I want you to warm my backside,
two S's snaked curve to curve
in the down burrow of the bed.

I want you to tuck in my illness,
coddle me with tea and chicken
soup whose steam sweetens the house.

I want you to watch my back
as the knives wink in the thin light
and the whips crack out from shelter.

Guard my body against dust and disuse,
warm me from the inside out,
lie over me, under me, beside me

in the bed as the night's creek
rushes over our shining bones
and we wake to the morning fresh

and wet, a birch leaf just uncurling.
Guard my body from disdain as age
widens me like a river delta.

Let us guard each other until death,
with teeth, brain and galloping heart,
each other's rose red warrior.

A PRECARIOUS BALANCE

Ancient wood

The wood speaks to me, said the carver,
I hear the song in it, of bear standing,
of wind shape that wants to cut through,
of snake undulating in the sand.

Wood is the stiff heart of the living
tree, the corpse left after its death.
We walk through our homes, our external
skeletons made of the bones of trees.

Some wood bends and some breaks.
Some we shape into baskets, wicker,
some into toothpicks, some into beams
that carry the weight of our lives.

But this petrified triangle beside
my computer is a different wonder:
an earthen hued rainbow of rock
shiny as ice, a knife once wood.

I could not carve it but it could
whittle me. I call it the poem
the wood made of its life, each
fat and lean year in shining rings.

The sugar and salts, the water
and sap are long transmuted
into a bright stone shape that has
outlasted not only tree but forest.

Blizzard in March

Thunder over the snowfields,
thunder cracking the ice
thin on the eel black river
winding in loops through the marsh.

The snow comes in sheets flapping.
The snow blinds me, matting
in my lashes, burning my eyes.
The cold is a metal tongue in my mouth.

In the house the yellow light
flickers and everything holds its breath.
No light, no heat, no water.
I am shaken like a paperweight.

Thunder throws chairs down the steps
of the sky. Snow thunder
like unexpected death,
the deer leaping into headlights

smashed across the splintering windshield.
Now lightning burns the snow:
the night divides into the terror
known and the fear not yet imagined.

March comes in on cleft hooves

I stand in my bedroom at blue dawn.
Superimposed on the pines, the supple wrists
of the dogwood with long buds swollen,
are my red Cretan wall hanging, my velvet
patchwork spread, my Victorian milk glass
bedside lamp at which the fawn appears
to sniff as she extends her swan neck.

We are in the same room of pale dreams,
the mother whose ears never stop snapping
back and forth, whose white tail twitches
at her flanks in its separate anxiety
while she grazes on wintergreen and bishop's
hat, has a little nibble on the peach tree.
Her daughter's eye gleams, caramel amber.

They come like a blessing into my bedroom,
only one pane of glass between them and us.
Woody and I hold hands, talking by touch
only, as she and her children bring March
in on velvet brows. Through the casement
cranked a crack, I hear the plaintive horns
of geese as they lift off beating north.

The visitation

The yearling doe stands by the pile of salt
hay, nibbling and then strolls up the path.
Among the forsythia she stands amazed,
hundreds of spring bulbs: daffodils,
the bright kiddush cups of tulips, crimson,
golden, orange streaked with green, the wild
tulips opening like stars fallen on the ground.
She leans gracefully to taste a tarda,
yellow and white sunburst, sees us, stops,
uncertain. Stares at us with her head cocked.
What are you? She is not frightened
but bemused. Do I know you?
The landscaping dazzles her, impresses her
far more than the two of us on the driveway
speaking to her in the same tone we use
with the cats as if she had become our pet,
as she sidles among the peach trees,
a pink blossom clinging to her dun flank.

Graceful among the rhododendron, I know
what her skittish courage represents: she
is beautiful as those sub-Saharan children
with the huge luminous brown eyes of star-
vation. A hard winter following a hurricane,

tangles of downed trees even the deer
cannot penetrate, a long slow spring
with the buds obdurate as pebbles,
too much building, so she comes to stand
in our garden, eyes flowering with wonder
under the incandescent buffet of the fruit
trees, this garden cafeteria she has walked
into to graze, from the lean late woods.

The voice of the grackle

Among the red-winged blackbirds—
latecomers clustered at the top
of the sugar maple after the others
have split up the better home sites
in the marshes, along Dun's Run—
their buzzes, chirs and warbles,
I hear a rasp, a harsh ruckus.

The grackles have come north again.
Nobody greets them with the joy
meted out to robins, the geese
rowing high overhead, the finches
flitting gold and red to the feeders.
I am their solitary welcoming
committee, tossing extra corn.

Their cries are no more melodious
than the screech of unadjusted
brakes, and yet I like their song
of the unoiled door hinge creaking,
the rusty saw grating, the squawk
of an air mattress stomped on,
unmistakable among the twitters.

They are big and shiny, handsome
even sulking in the rain.
Feathers gleam like the polish

on a new car when the sun hits them,
black as asphalt, with oil slick
colors shimmering, purple satin
like hoods in their gang colors.

We never see more than a few,
often one alone, like the oversized
kid who hangs out, misfit, with
the younger crowd, slumps at the back
of the classroom making off color
comments in his cracking voice,
half clown, half hero.

Thousands of morning moths

Today in the early June woods
the green surged around us, rustling
at full reach, the water at high
tide in every stem and leaf,
all leaves bright as jellies.

As we walked the twisting sand road
beside the hidden river where green
frogs tweaked their cello strings,
hundreds of white butterflies
the size of thumb nails showered

past us, flitting among the multiflora
rose bowed with new leaves and buds
but not yet showing a single petal
but for these, like a dance
of petals falling from the apple.

No matter that they gnaw trees bare
as hairy caterpillars: scattered now
on the June dawn, they are a blessing
following us over dew beaded grass
along the road like friendly laughter.

In June, the young deer
are almost tame

We had met the two of them, young mates.
She was the more curious, tame.
The smell of oils and linseed drew her.
Once I saw her standing behind a painter
at the side of the sand road, looking
over his shoulder like a tourist pausing.

In the early morning we often saw them
as we did this morning. He ran across
the paved road by the dike, she
followed, and the new station wagon
driven by a doctor with Georgia plates
came roaring over the hill far too fast.

He hit her so hard she went high in the air,
landed on his windshield, stumbled
forward, then lay kicking. He paused,
started away. I stood before him
flagging him down, but he would not
get out. He drove off, left us with her.

I knelt by her, still thrashing,
the blood now blooming from her mouth,
running in a brilliant stream
a touch of fuchsia in the scarlet.
I had to help her die. I cradled
the beautiful head, eyes wide in terror,

I closed the windpipe with my hands.
She was bleeding so hard that

my execution was fast. Within two
minutes, she was still and her open
eye glazed over and the sweet tawny
flank was still at last.

She was the color of my Siamese Arofa
whom I had to help to die fourteen
years ago. I could not let the vet
kill her. She would have known.
She could read our emotions
like captions on a foreign movie.

I think of an old man lying
in a hospital bed, his legs cut off,
his head smashed in, and the tubes
and the machines keeping him from quiet.
I have been close enough to death
to know that there is a time

when life is indistinguishable from pain,
when you want to turn your face
to the wall and pass through it
into fog that slowly lifts on the wind
and goes into the air and the earth,
each molecule becoming something else.

There is a time to be other.
But death can spring without warning,
pretext, the great thing that strikes
in the middle of a morning when the locust

trees are hung with great honeyed
bunches of sweet flowers to graze,

when every leaf is still fresh and sweet,
when the multiflora roses turn
the sand roads into bowers of perfume,
you smashed and gasping with pain,
me having to play Dr. Death, pressing
your maiden throat in my shaking hands.

Death of a doe on Chequesset Neck

Because you did not look at what
you had done, because you sped
off while she lay bleeding,
you learned nothing.
You are empty as a new computer.

What you kill you must look
at, what you kill
you must embrace, going
with your victim partway
into the trapdoor in the ground.

Her blood flowed in rivulets
past me. I held her long
Gothic head. Her death
was in my hands. Her wide
eyes met mine, locking.

I shut off the pain with the
breath till her eyes jelled.
In my hands her life flowed
like the blood in spasms
of energy pulsing, light

burning into my palms.
Pain passed into me and the green
life running in the June woods
white with drooping locust blossoms,
wet with rain and blood.

The sky changes

I watch the dry wind chafing
the clay cliffs at the bay.

The sand scoots in ghosts
across the sliced open visage

of history and carves it off,
so the striated cliff crumbles.

Peavines wither and yellow, frogs
stretch parched in the white dust.

The pump labors like a miner
with emphysema, dry coughing.

The velvet of the roses is dusty.
Flesh is sandpaper and onionskin.

Our sex grates. We come in dust.
Old smells paint the air brown.

After a musty dank afternoon
the color of mold on peaches,

distant thunder muttering curses
rolling away, at last rain.

Now the sluice gates of the clouds
open and the sky falls on us.

Slowly as the rain enters us,
we swell, every drought-sucked leaf.

Afterward all the birds rise singing
and the fruits of the vine,

tomato and grape, zucchini and cucumber
are huge and cool and succulent.

Our bed rocks on the waves of the rain
and we drink each other, quenched.

A quick and quiet one

1

I watch the garter snake thrust
itself forward across the sand road
and into the bearberry, motion
flowing along it like peristalsis.

Nothing moves on two or four legs,
on wings or fins or flippers
more gracefully than this belly
to the dust creature that suffers,

dies from our mindless loathing.
On my palm you feel dry, warm
as the sand, muscular, tasting
the air with your tongue

staring at me, curious, not
struggling but savoring the touch
of my hand as I relax into stroking
your intricate mosaic.

You have a kind of Byzantine
formality rearing to inspect me.
I put you down and you whip off,
tracing S's through the bronze grass.

2

Often we use animals as distorting
mirrors, our ferocity in the wolf,
our lust in the rabbit, the tomcat,
our duplicity in the fox and coyote.

But in the snake we encounter
the other we cannot dress in Disney
short pants or bouffant skirts.
We see a stranger slipping

quick as water down a hole,
or basking on a rock, ancient
eye slitted, the body moving
supple coil on coil of strength.

We look at this belly dancer
and we see death, we see deceit
with an angel face garlanded
upon the tree that made us human.

We see everything except that swift
archaic beauty brushing over the earth
with an intimacy we cannot
imagine, seeking warmth and prey.

Crow babies

The crows are scolding the hunters.
The crows are calling me out
under the oaks to attend to them.
They like me, I am useful,
they flap near my shoulders and feet
large as dogs with wings.
They are always on patrol.

They bless me.
They let me hear them sing
an opera in the pitch pines.
They have many cries
and their eyes are jackknives
and their feathers carved
of obsidian and rainbows.

They raise their children
on my land, another blessing.
This year I watched them teaching
flight, big awkward children
like overgrown corner boys
cursing at top decibel,
tumbling, ruffled, pissed.

Why do we have to learn this,
they kept complaining, why
can't you go on feeding us?
Do you want to crawl like her,

the parents, the aunts,
the grandmothers mocked them,
when men chase you, you'll fly.

I scatter corn in the winter.
They squat on my compost pile
steaming into the snow and jeer
at lesser birds and tell ribald
jokes and laugh. They ignore
my cats who ignore them.
Now the year's offspring

are furled into huge black
umbrellas, bumbershoots, dressed
the same as their parents
like Hasids. They share food,
they post guards, they fight
owls together: a better society
in the interstices of ours.

The level

A great balance hangs in the sky
and briefly on the black pan
and on the blue pan, the melon
of the moon and the blood orange
of the sun are symmetrical
like two unmatched eyes glowing
at us with one desire.

This is an instant's equality,
a level that at once
starts to dip. In spring
the sun starts up its golden
engine earlier each dawn.
In fall, night soaks
its dye into the edges of day.

But now they hang, two bright
balls teasing us to balance
the halves of our brain, need
and will, gut and intellect,
you and me in an instant's grace—
understanding no woman, even
Gaia, can always make it work.

October eclipse

Tonight she does not glow.
Darkness eats at her,
as if two whole weeks of waning
were speeded up before us.

An eclipse of the sun
feels dangerous. Darkness
spreads unnaturally.
The birds go to sleep.

The wind rises cold
as if from a cavern.
All things imagine death.
The sun hides its face

but shows us its fiery
hair, the mane of corona.
Then dawn comes three
hundred sixty degrees

around and the birds
start up their racket.
The wind slackens.
You feel silly.

But the moon slides
into darkness without threats.

Instead she becomes
a copper mirror, a dim

glass showing us ourselves.
It is we who shine now
reflected off her.
I return you to yourself,

she sings in the dark
of our shadow falling,
see how you too are
beings of cool light.

Off season rental

The sea turns over on its side
kicking the belly of the dune.
In this old rented house every floor
board groans with a different
betrayal. The wind fills up
its pockets with sand and empties
them on the porch. It tries
each shingle grey as a mouse
and bangs one shutter upstairs
in a vanished bedroom
where someone died complaining.

The wind uses the dune grass
as compasses to draw circles
on the chalky glinting sand.
You wake in the morning weary
as if you had marched all night,
a forced decampment to the black
marshes where the night herons
hunt snakes. You feel sure
a relentless voice has been
eroding your eardrums all night
gossiping of Civil War captains.

The space between the inner
and outer walls is stuffed with hundred
year old newspapers and words,

promises of love, threats, schemes
dried and powdery as old seaweed.
One morning in the kitchen a dog
is waiting to be fed and then
slowly vanishes like fog
that sits on the sand bar briefly.
Last to fade are reproachful eyes
and the silently beating tail.

Trying our metal

Silver I like better than gold
not just for the moony glint
but because it tarnishes.

Some metals outlast us centuries.
Dig them up from the earth,
a gold hoard, aluminum,

wash them and they shine new.
Silver is always going back
to the air, aging dark.

I like the kinship of iron,
iron that dissolves in water
staining porcelain under the tap,

iron that rides the little cars
of the red cells through our blood,
iron that turns orange as it leaks

into the air, softens in weather,
iron that finally crumbles like bones
back into the soil that reluctantly

gave it up to the fire.
We too dissolve in the slow caustic
wash of the river of years.

Transfixed on the bank

All rivers are mysteries.
Like train tracks they connote
passage and abandonment.
It depends on whether you stand
on the bank or push off.

The bottom is usually hidden,
rock or mud, three feet down
or forty, only the slowest
and shallowest will let
the soles of your feet read them.

All are going somewhere,
rivers and streams and creeks,
going and going. They say,
let go. Open your fists.
Let it slide out of you.

Eddies furl in the current.
Pools yawn and wink.
Water riffles over the hidden bar.
A snag sticks up bony.
The sound hurries you along.

But you stand still watching
different water pass the same
place. Time feels circular
but isn't. Its wide river bears
us downstream and out to sea.

Syzygy

*Either of two points in the moon's orbit when it lies in
a straight line with the sun and the earth, or the sun,
the moon and the earth lined up.*

Sometimes I drift in a precarious balance,
caught between opposing pulls,
turning on my own axis in peace
created of contradiction and cross-purpose
able to find in the war of worlds
a place of my own intent.

At times great forces pull in alignment,
the cold and the burning, what gives life
and what sucks it up, what creates
and what remembers, what lures us into sleep
and the subterranean twilight of dreams.

Then both the night and the day
sing together and call the ocean
high high up pawing the cliffs, gouging
the clay with deep claw marks,
drawing the water far into the marsh.
Moon ripples on what was a meadow
where wavelets prick and glint.

My womb and my mind open and bleed.
I am played like a trumpet flat out,

a sursum corda without consent, regret,
without a quibble or reflection,
an instrument of the planet.

Then that moment of pure compulsion
we call the muse slips into normal
conflict, resolution, and I contemplate
my own center again, wobbling a little
between my wandering poles.

MY BOA

My boa

What says home is various as the shades
of earth, red clay, white sand,
mahogany loam, mica and granite.

It was during the Vietnam bloodbath.
A young woman named Faith came to us
from Christian communists in Paraguay

via England where she had been studying
and where she had insulted the prime
minister during a church service

(regarded by her as obscene)
by protesting with a bloody banner.
We were hiding her from Interpol

on the fringes of Bedford-Stuyvesant
in Brooklyn, in an old brownstone
occupied by an Indian couple

and two floors of SDS activists.
A Jew and an atheist, we fed her
and kept her safe, a big blond strapping

young woman with hair of pale hemp
devout as my grandmother had been.
She demanded an outing in summer.

We decided the Bronx Zoo was safe.

We stopped by the new world monkeys.
She pointed. "That kind is delicious.

We used to fry them in the jungle."
But when we came to the boa constrictors
vast somnolent green monsters,

tears slid from her eyes. Voice
thickened, she cooed to them. "Oh,
I miss home. I miss my mother."

She had trapped the big snakes
for zoos and collectors. They
lived as pets in the family compound.

She hung over the pit of serpents
weeping and we had to drag her away
from the staring, dangerous crowd.

It is the taste of a ripe tomato
full of the juice of the sun, that sings
to me this evening in Lyon, of a garden

by the sea, of my bed, of my cats
and friends: my own sweet place
where work waits like a boa constrictor

but my own vast green coiling monster,
my own.

If we can't find it, we make it

I remember lying in the grass of the yard
staring at the bricks that edged the border
of flowers, black eyed susans, chrysanthemums,

purple iris, and every chipped brick housed
cities of brown ants. I thought the race of ants
lived in adobe pueblos I had seen in a photo.

I remember staring into the wood of the bed board,
swirling maple eddying into pools. I saw landscapes,
relief maps of mountain forests I wandered in.

Every textured object hatched miniature worlds,
the ceiling, the flowered drapes, illustrations
in books, as if reality were a sieve

through which leaked intimations of elsewhere.
Think of the rat grey street, the asphalt alley,
the air oily with coal smoke, brown rain

acid enough to etch bone. Dirty frame houses
leaned on their elbows over the street.
Tell me why I saw crystalline seas in bottles.

The world from below

To a young child, all grown-ups are tall,
all rooms stretch into skies of ceiling
you study. You are always lying on your

back so you walk the ceilings, stepping
over the high doorways. The windows
are just the right level for you to stare out.

There's no big furniture crouching
but light fixtures like flowers in the center
of the white emptiness where you dance.

Under the diningroom table you crawl,
staring up at the pale underside while the lace
hangs down making you a tent of power.

You run little plastic cars up the claw legs.
There are tunnels in the walls only the mice
know, where they emerge by the hot air

registers. Every mark on the walls speaks
to you, eyes and fish, bats and wild horses.
Under the easy chairs dust moss hangs.

The bathroom tiles repeat and repeat
like a loud clock. You study every crack,
decoding the world secretly, and wrong.

Growing up haunted

When I enter through the hatch of memory
those claustrophobic chambers,
my adolescence in the booming fifties
of General Eisenhower, General Foods
and General Motors, I see our dreams:
obsolescent mannequins in Dior frocks,
armored, prefabricated bodies;
and I see our nightmares, powerful
as a wine red sky and wall of fire.

Fear was the underside of every leaf
we turned, the knowledge that our
cousins, our other selves, had been
starved and butchered to ghosts.
The question every smoggy morning
presented like a covered dish:
why are you living and all those
mirror selves, sisters, gone
into smoke like stolen cigarettes?

I remember my grandmother's cry
when she learned the death of all she
remembered, girls she bathed with,
young men with whom she shyly
flirted, wooden shul where
her father rocked and prayed,

red haired aunt plucking the
balalaika, world of sun and snow
turned to shadows on a yellow page.

Assume no future you may not have
to fight for, to die for, muttered
ghosts gathered on the foot
of my bed each night. What you
carry in your blood is us,
the books we did not write,
music we could not make, a world
gone from gristle to smoke, only
as real now as words can make it.

The flying Jew

I never met Uncle Dave.
The most real thing I know about him
is how he died, which he did
again and again in the middle of the night
my mother screaming, my father shouting,
Shut up, Bert, you're having a bad dream.

My Uncle Dave, the recurring nightmare.
He was the Jew who flew.
How did he manage it? Flying was for
gentlemen, and he was a kid from the slums
of Philadelphia, Pittsburgh, Cleveland—
zaydeh one headlong leap ahead of the law
and the Pinkertons, the goons who finally
bashed his head in when he was organizing
his last union, the bakery workers.

Dave looked up between the buildings,
higher than the filthy sparrows who pecked
at horse dung and the pigeons who strutted
and cooed in the tenement eaves,
up to the grey clouds of Philadelphia,
the rust clouds of Pittsburgh with the fires
of the open hearth steel mills staining them,
a pillar of smoke by day and fire by night.

He followed into the clouds.
My mother doesn't even know who taught

him to fly, but he learned.
He became one with the plane, they said.
Off he went to France. He flew in combat,
was shot down and survived, never
became an ace, didn't enjoy combat,
the killing, but flying was better than sex.

He took my mother up once and she wept
the whole time. She wouldn't fly again
till she was seventy-five and said then
she didn't care if the plane went down.

It was his only talent, his only passion
and a good plane was a perfect fit for
his body and his mind, his reflexes.
The earth was something that clung to his shoes,
something to shake off, something to gather
all your strength into a taut charge
and then launch forward and leave behind.

After the war, he was lost for two years,
tried selling, tried insurance, then off
he went barnstorming with his war buddies.
Time on the ground was just stalling time,

killing time, parked in roominghouses
and tourist homes and bedbug hotels.
He drank little. Women were aspirin.

Being the only Jew, he had something
to prove every day, so he flew the fastest,
he did the final trick that made the audience
shriek. The planes grew older, the crowds
thinned out. One fall day outside Cleveland
he got his mother, sister Bert and her
little boy to watch the act. It was a triple
Immelmann roll he had done five hundred
shows but this time the plane plowed
into the earth and a fireball rose.

So every six months he died flaming
in the middle of the night, and all I
ever knew of him was Mother screaming.

My rich uncle, whom I only met three times

We were never invited to his house.
We went there once while they were all in Hawaii,
climbed steps from which someone had shoveled
the snow, not him, to the wide terrace.
Yellow brick, the house peered into fir and juniper.
It was too large for me to imagine what it held
but I was sure every one of them, four girls
and bony wife, each had a room of her own.

He had been a magician and on those rare
nights he had to stay at the Detroit Statler
downtown, he would summon us for supper
in the hotel restaurant. Mother would put on
and take off every dress in her closet, all six,
climb in the swaybacked brown Hudson muttering shame.
He would do tricks with his napkin and pull
quarters from my ears and spoons from his sleeves.

He had been a clumsy acrobat, he had failed at comedy
and vaudeville; he was entertaining for a party
when he met a widow with four girls and an inheritance.
He waltzed right out of her romantic movie dreams
and he strolled into her house and she had him redone.
He learned to talk almost like her dead husband.
He learned to wear suits, order dinners and give orders

to servants. His name changed, his background rebuilt,
his religion painted over, he almost fit in.

Of my uncles, only he was unreal, arriving by plane
to stay on the fanciest street in downtown Detroit.
The waiter brought a phone to the table, his broker
calling. I imagined a cowboy breaking horses.
He made knives disappear. He made a napkin vanish.
He was like an animated suit, no flesh, no emotions
bubbling the blood and steaming the windows as
my other uncles and aunts did. Only the discreet
Persian leather smell of money droned in my nose.

His longest trick was to render his past invisible.
Then one night after the guests had left, he went down
to the basement in the latest multi-level glass vast
whatnot shelf of house and hanged himself by the furnace.
They did not want his family at the funeral. She had
no idea, his wife said, why would he be depressed?
I remember his laugh like a cough and his varnished
face, buffed till the silverware shone in his eyes.
His last trick was to vanish himself forever.

On the road in middle age

Hell is traveling forever
from bad hotel to disgusting B & B,
from the motel where the towels
feel used and the carpet
is woe colored and smells of roach poison,
to the B & B reeking of cabbage
where the toilet is in the bedroom,
and plumbing vibrates like a jet engine,
to the hotel without air conditioning
across the street from the all
night gay bar and the dawn depot.

At twenty, you slept on a door
mat and rose to marvel at the sun
rising remarkably still in the east.
At twenty, you could sleep through
earthquakes, thrill at bedbugs,
munch bread and chocolate and oranges
and call it breakfast and dinner.
You camped by the road drinking
lukewarm bitter wine and waited
for a ride six hours in the rain.

Now you are always repacking.
At every stop you lose a brush
or stocking or button.
You have too much luggage
heavy as bags of bowling balls

but you wear only the same
tired sweater day after day.
Indigestion is constant as
the rain, the mud.

You are always trying to change
tickets in a foreign language.
Even the birds sing melodies
you can't recognize. Signs
warn you of incomprehensible
dangers. You consult your
pocket dictionary, but the words
that matter are never there.

Diana inaccessible

for Diana der Hovanessian

Must we always measure values
in terms of loss?
With you gone off, inaccessible
in a mythical country

named Armenia where real people
bleed and rot, where everything
but pain is scarce,
where mail awaits a second coming,

I find I miss you not
occasionally, now and the
odd Thursday or wet Wednesday
but as if some vital connection

to my brain were yanked out.
You have become my muse.
When I write a poem, I know
I'll share it with you.

I am truthful with you
to a fault, delivering
troubles to your door
like a load of coal to the cellar.

I have this odd sense of loose
ends, wires dangling, an accumulated
looseleaf of addenda to my life,
collected for your homecoming.

Reflections on a mirror

Mirror mirror on the wall
Bathroom mirror in which I sought
to catch my own nakedness
at twelve as black hair
began to tangle like briars
over the triangle where my thighs
met, mirror where my early breasts
gleamed absurd as lemons.

Mirror in which I would glimpse
sometimes another world under
lying this one, a shadow
world of grey women peering
over my shoulder, a world
where light broke in waves
on the windows of morning,
where night's chocolate melted.

Mirror to which I said NO,
I will not be sucked thin by you
like a sour candy. I will
not fall into your dim waters
and drown in my own eyes,
I will not seek my smirk
in you as I pass through
restaurants, parties, halls.

Mirror where I stood with candles
burning on either side and promised
myself I would dive through

appearances into the dark waters
lapping beneath you, all the way
down into the octopus cave
where I would seize my own self
like a precious living conch.

Now I have aged in you
like something softening under
water, a gradual blurring
of lines and boundaries.
You have little left to give me
yet I love how you capture light
and fling it back. In you
the world turns half around.

The descent of Orphée

Blue flame cupped
in the fragile bowl of the body,
I will not give you over to oblivion.
I will not let you dissolve in the wet
acid of failing memory.

I go into the pit.
Cold and dark, I am buffeted
by dank winds that strip the skin from me.
My hair blanches to Spanish moss
and tears off in dull hanks.
Like Inanna gone into the underworld,
I am becoming a corpse.

Still the mind watches, the eyes are
terribly open and seeing
as Damiens, who tried to kill hated King Louis,
was still talking after his arms
and legs had been pulled from his body.
The myth has it wrong.
The dissection and the descent are one.

We go down, we go down into the pit,
each of us, alone and never alone,
haunted by everyone we have loved,
everyone we have wounded and maimed.
We go down into the bloody maelstrom

where slowly the winds take us apart
spar by lath by shattering glass.

I go to fight death for the beloved.
I will not let her go into darkness
and dissolution. I will not let
his face wear smooth as an old coin
till the profile is any face.
I will not let their names
vanish like signs weathered white
in the weeds beside a winding road
the superhighway has bypassed.

I go to charm death like Scheherazade
with stories that I refuse to end
until my wish is granted.
There in the womb of the winds
I begin to rebuild Eurydice, eyelashes
pale as spider silk, eyes
bold and bright as a jay,
a crow's laughter, hands of water
and ice, I begin to rebuild her.

I am leading her out, a step, a step
a phrase at a time, she is being
embodied. I hear her breath now,

now her steps shuffling
as if through fallen leaves.

We are almost up. My own body
is re-forming. I see my hand
flesh again cradling the bones.
Then as the first light gives color
to the thick and thin of the dark,
I dare to turn. There is no body.
Only a book flies past me
into the light.

The mean

The grungy truth is, there is relief
in being a middle aged orphan. We
would talk Mondays, when he, *your
father,* never *my husband,*
was playing bridge or poker.
She would weep for hours. *He
stands over me while I vacuum,
he tells me how to make beds.*

Coercion and despair, and the ground
swell underneath, *Save me,
take me away,* yet every suggestion
she dismissed. *I can't do that.
I'm too old. I can't drive.
No one would listen to me.*
It took me years to understand:
complaining is a kind of soul song.

Her blood pressure rose like a tube
of jelly squeezed in a great hand.
I sent packages of health food,
directions, vitamins, meditation
tapes: after her death, I found
them all in the high kitchen
cabinet where she did not have
to look at them, ever.

Then his seams started opening.
I never knew when the calls
would come, 3 a.m., 4 a.m.,

You've stolen my pencils!
The calls in the daytime, he
hasn't paid his bills, he owes
taxes, he went outside naked
again. He became a cartoon.

The sordid truth is, after the grief,
relief. No more making the money
stretch all year, Hamburger Helper.
I balanced coercion and despair,
habits of a lifetime beating against
mean rules of a bureaucracy,
the casual dirt of a man used
to a body servant called a wife.

For the last decade of their lives,
I was on call; I was the distant
night nurse; I was the cavalry
taking the late flight south
to barge into the Social Security
office, to hire the lawyer, to
threaten the supervisor, to stage
a perfect tantrum in the right office.

We dump the old into fluorescent
dustbins. At the end, all preserved
angers simply dry to grey husks.
There you are dragging someone who
can't remember who you are, whose mind
has kited into nineteen forty-two,

in to see a doctor who despises him,
gives him pills like punishment.

After ten years, I still hear her voice,
am brought up short at a closed door.
He was an irascible king-size baby
in diapers, banging the walls of his pen.
Eskimos setting the old adrift on the ice
are kinder. Show me the way through.
I couldn't find it. A deficit
of love from beginning to end.

Kaddish

Look around us, search above us, below, behind.
We stand in a great web of being joined together.
Let us praise, let us love the life we are lent
passing through us in the body of Israel
and our own bodies, let's say amen.

Time flows through us like water.
The past and the dead speak through us.
We breathe out our children's children, blessing.

Blessed is the earth from which we grow,
blessed the life we are lent,
blessed the ones who teach us,
blessed the ones we teach,
blessed is the word that cannot say the glory
that shines through us and remains to shine
flowing past distant suns on the way to forever.
Let's say amen.

Blessed is light, blessed is darkness,
but blessed above all else is peace
which bears the fruits of knowledge
on strong branches, let's say amen.

Peace that bears joy into the world,
peace that enables love, peace over Israel
everywhere, blessed and holy is peace, let's say amen.

Season of breakage

1

The hurricane parched the oak leaves brown,
stripped the luckier trees to broken twigs.
Others it tore up by the roots, tossed on roofs
and cars, used to tangle electric wires
like spaghetti twirled around a fork.
A grove of locusts became a plain of stumps.

For the rest of August we moved through
the low hills, the marshes of late November,
leafless under the roaring full maned sun,
landscape brown above the waist while the ground
was green, the low protected bushes still
offering their season's growth and berries.

Now the earth has gone mad with confusion.
Brown leaves drift, buds splitting above.
The crabapple offers its lush pink blossoms
clashing with leaves turning scarlet.
Lilacs bloom along Ryder Beach Road
where the Virginia creeper glows crimson.

The surviving locusts are white with panicles
of blossom set against the leaves' still unspent
lime green coins the wind tells over.
This is an unkempt unnerving beauty,
a pageant whose cost we cannot measure
till after the winter has taxed us lean.

2

We are cheated of fall. Only the low
bushes and the ground covers brighten.
Poison ivy, blueberry, hog cranberry
are right and red on the calendar clock.

Anything as tall as a person is conned,
confused, trying to start all over again
when they should be battening down,
hunkered for the ripping blast of winter.

After disaster we too fly in mad circles
as terrified horses dash back into
the burning barn. We think we can force
time back, return to the moment whose promise

distilled in the nose its ripe aroma
of matured hope. If we say the magic
words of pleading and pledge, the lover
will lie down in our bed shivering desire.

It is the Medusa head that freezes us
at the crossroads, looking vainly back
to the golden haze of ignorance before
catastrophe, but we are years older

than yesterday, we are somebody else
whose blood has burned like oil all night,

whose bones have hardened, darkened
to mahogany in the salt cured flesh.

Our virtue is to become wise as gods,
knowing we are helpless as maggots,
and go on out of the burning house
into the winter that will kill or renew us.

After the wind abated, he walked out and died

for Arne Manos (1941–1991)

A little green snake trapped
like a silken braid
in the hands, quick jerk
of the supple spine
and it glides free
gone into the camouflage grass.

Blue eyes of the dayflower
weed among the alyssum
like the hemerocallis
opens each day its fresh flower
that fades and withers
with the bleeding sun.

I would have eaten more chocolate
if I'd known said the dying
woman, I would have told all
my affection, I would have lain
reading the worry beads of his spine
an hour to each.

But we do know.
The clock face opens and
closes its scissor hands
cutting us from the minute

the hour that never
comes back.

The watch in our chest keeps
time for us—keeps? No,
spends the time as it runs through
us on its millipede legs.
This is our longest dance, but we
lose the patterns we are casting.

We die always in the moment
like a book falling shut
and the story is finished except
for those resonances that darken
in the minds of others, toward silence
and the long cold between the stars.

Season of the egg

It's the season of the egg,
older than any named creed:
that perfect shape that signs
a pregnant woman, the moon

slightly compressed, as if
a great serpent held it
in its opened mouth
to carry or eat.

Eggs smell funky
slipped from under
the hen's breast, hotter
than our blood.

Christians paint them;
we roast them. The only
time in the whirling year
I ever eat roasted egg:

a campfire flavor, bit
burnt, reeking of haste
like the matzoh there was no
time to let rise.

We like our eggs honest,
brown. Outside my window

the chickadees choose partners
to lay tiny round eggs.

The egg of the world cracks
raggedly open and the wet
scraggly chick of northern
spring emerges gaunt, dripping.

Soon it will preen its green
feathers, soon it will grow
fat and strong, its wings
blue and blinding.

Tonight we dip the egg in salt
water like bowls of tears.
Elijah comes with the fierce
early spring bringing prophecy

that cracks open the head
swollen with importance.
Every day there is more work
to do and stronger light.

Matzoh

Flat you are as a door mat
and as homely.
No crust, no glaze, you lack
a cosmetic glow.
You break with a snap.
You are dry as a twig
split from an oak
in midwinter.
You are bumpy as a mud basin
in a drought.
Square as a slab of pavement,
you have no inside
to hide raisins or seeds.
You are pale as the full moon
pocked with craters.

What we see is what we get,
honest, plain, dry
shining with nostalgia
as if baked with light
instead of heat.
The bread of flight and haste
in the mouth you
promise, home.

A twitch in time

The cat knows something.
See how her ears flatten
as she listens to a sound
so sinister her fur stands
in a wind of wariness.

The sky knows something
taking on a red glow
as if a fire burned
behind those metal clouds.
They might be smoke.

The crow suspects,
rasping warnings that scrape
the air raw, chafed with menace
then flapping off like a black flag.
Even the crow abandons her nest.

Something is gathering force.
Somewhere an earthen dam
of circumstance that protected
invisibly upstream has sprung
cracks like lines on a palm

that can be read, danger, danger.
Somewhere the water is piling
up in the dark, roiling,

thrashing. Cracks widening,
that nameless dam buckles.

Downstream the nape itches,
a cat twitches as if bitten,
a crow flees on the rising wind,
and a woman clutches herself at a window
waiting for the stranger to walk in.

Targets

I am shooting targets propped against
a sandy bank in Wellfleet woods.
The cataract in my eye pours
dirty canal water over the scene.
I have not seen a clear blue in months.
I shoot from instinct only
not telling my instructor
how it goes with me.

This is a hand gun.
I learned to shoot a rifle.
The men who taught me to shoot are dead.
I remember the shock to my shoulder,
the impact that felt like necessity
itself slamming into me.
I thought because it hurt
it was more real.

This is a nice man,
good to his failing mother and me.
He guesses I am going blind.
He served in Vietnam.
In a war like the old one I was
fighting those years I learned
to shoot, we would be
on opposite sides.

It is as if the gun is
an extension of my arm.
I point at things and point again.
I remember a hillside of rocks

like exclamation points
dry as the moon
hot as a black car in the sun,
sweat, laughter and rum.

I am a point of memory
like a seed that might
hatch a bean plant or a cactus.
I carry in me landscapes of the dead,
old lost wars, danger
jolting the brain like a hot
wire, while I shoot at small
painted targets in the sand.

The price begins to mount

What gets you in its teeth in middle age
is not what we had imagined. Sex is perhaps
easier, less fraught, less imagined,
common and rich and something the body
has learned to do with another like tennis
but deeper and longer in its mind body meld.

Years ago in Denmark I struck my left elbow.
Some mornings it suddenly sings of rain and morbidity.
The Nazis who kneecapped me in Central Park under
the Viet Cong flag come back to me in their ferocity
when one bright morning translucent as a light gel
it gives under me, the ground rising to strike me.

It is the dizziness that presses with a heavy hand
on my head, bowing me toward my soft belly.
It is the organs you never knew you had singing out,
a liver, a gallbladder, adrenals, one evening
knocking you down the steps or turning your blood
to a viscid grey liquid that coats the eyes blind.

It is the moment the bad genes combine and come
on line, Hi there, this is Grandma's cancer reporting
from your stomach, the glaucoma of the father
who scarcely remembered your name stealing
your vision like a sneak, filing your optic nerve
to fraying while you sleep.

Half the population reads astrology columns
in the paper, the TV Guide, yet we ignore
what is encoded in the genes tucked into each cell

tinier than the writing in mezuzahs.
Always we are shocked when a new trouble
Aunt Harriet had when we were seven kicks in.

Maybe your mother left you a jade necklace,
her ring, but this is the true inheritance,
cataracts dimming your vision and the tendency
to have your brain crack open with a stroke.
This is the real will your father produced,
that time bomb ticking in your chest like a heart.

The world unbandaged

Slowly after the pain my vision came
and light entered me like a careful lover.
Gradually around me the world settled
its wings and became clear and still.

And I woke in the morning and opened
my eyes and I saw. Colors sang
like a Verdi opera, every
hue a diva, a world class tenor.

I rose in the day clothed in glitter
like a peacock of fire and I saw
each tree shining with its leaves
like pulsating green hearts.

I saw the face of my lover again
his sea colored eyes, his mouth
speaking to me, it was truly him
and his countenance of sun.

Around me the world was busy
with itself like a mother cat
washing her kittens, and the morning
bubbled with inner and outer light.

Coming up on September

White butterflies, with single
black fingerpaint eyes on their wings
dart and settle, eddy and mate
over the green tangle of vines
in Labor Day morning steam.

The year grinds into ripeness
and rot, grapes darkening,
pears yellowing, the first
Virginia creeper twining crimson,
the grasses, dry straw to burn.

The New Year rises, beckoning
across the umbrellas on the sand.
I begin to reconsider my life.
What is the yield of my impatience?
What is the fruit of my resolve?

I turn from my frantic white dance
over the jungle of productivity
and slowly a niggun slides,

cold water down my throat.
I rest on a leaf spotted red.

Now is the time to let the mind
search backwards like the raven loosed
to see what can feed us. Now,
the time to cast the mind forward
to chart an aerial map of the months.

The New Year is a great door
that stands across the evening and Yom
Kippur is the second door. Between them
are song and silence, stone and clay pot
to be filled from within myself.

I will find there both ripeness and rot,
what I have done and undone,
what I must let go with the waning days
and what I must take in. With the last
tomatoes, we harvest the fruit of our lives.

Breadcrumbs

Some time on Rosh Hashana I go,
a time dictated by tide charts,
services. The once I did tashlich

on the rising tide and the crumbs
floated back to me, my energy soured,
vinegar of anxiety. Now I eye the times.

I choose the dike, where the Herring River
pours in and out of the bay, where at
low tide in September blue herons stalk

totemic to spear the alewives hastening
silver-sided from the fresh ponds to
the sea. As I toss my crumbs, muttering

prayers, a fisherman rebukes me: It's
not right to feed the fish, it distracts
them from his bait. Sometimes

it's odd to be a Jew, like a three-
legged heron with bright purple head,
an ibis in white plumes diving

except that with global warming
we do sometimes glimpse an ibis
in our marshes, and I am rooted here

to abide the winter when this tourist
has gone back to Cincinnati.
My rituals are mated to this fawn

colored land floating on the horizon
of water. My havurah calls itself
Am ha-Yam, people of the sea,

and we are wedded to the ocean
as truly as the Venetian doge who tossed
his gold ring to the Adriatic.

All rivers flow at last into the sea
but here it is, at once. So we stand
the tourist casting for his fish

and I tossing my bread. The fish
snap it up. Tonight perhaps
he will broil my sins for supper.

The art of blessing the day

This is the blessing for rain after drought:
Come down, wash the air so it shimmers,
a perfumed shawl of lavender chiffon.
Let the parched leaves suckle and swell.
Enter my skin, wash me for the little
chrysalis of sleep rocked in your plashing.
In the morning the world is peeled to shining.

This is the blessing for sun after long rain:
Now everything shakes itself free and rises.
The trees are bright as pushcart ices.
Every last lily opens its satin thighs.
The bees dance and roll in pollen
and the cardinal at the top of the pine
sings at full throttle, fountaining.

This is the blessing for a ripe peach:
This is luck made round. Frost can nip
the blossom, kill the bee. It can drop,
a hard green useless nut. Brown fungus,
the burrowing worm that coils in rot can
blemish it and wind crush it on the ground.
Yet this peach fills my mouth with juicy sun.

This is the blessing for the first garden tomato:
Those green boxes of tasteless acid the store
sells in January, those red things with the savor
of wet chalk, they mock your fragrant name.
How fat and sweet you are weighing down my palm,

warm as the flank of a cow in the sun.
You are the savor of summer in a thin red skin.

This is the blessing for a political victory:
Although I shall not forget that things
work in increments and epicycles and sometime
leaps that half the time fall back down,
let's not relinquish dancing while the music
fits into our hips and bounces our heels.
We must never forget, pleasure is real as pain.

The blessing for the return of a favorite cat,
the blessing for love returned, for friends'
return, for money received unexpected,
the blessing for the rising of the bread,
the sun, the oppressed. I am not sentimental
about old men mumbling the Hebrew by rote
with no more feeling than one says gesundheit.

But the discipline of blessings is to taste
each moment, the bitter, the sour, the sweet
and the salty, and be glad for what does not
hurt. The art is in compressing attention
to each little and big blossom of the tree
of life, to let the tongue sing each fruit,
its savor, its aroma and its use.

Attention is love, what we must give
children, mothers, fathers, pets,
our friends, the news, the woes of others.

What we want to change we curse and then
pick up a tool. Bless whatever you can
with eyes and hands and tongue. If you
can't bless it, get ready to make it new.

A note about the author

Marge Piercy is the author of eighteen previous poetry collections, a memoir, seventeen novels, a book of short stories, and four nonfiction books. Her work has been translated into twenty-one languages, and she has won many honors, including the Golden Rose, the oldest poetry award in the country. She lives on Cape Cod with her husband, Ira Wood, the novelist, memoirist, community radio interviewer, and essayist. She has given readings, lectures, or workshops at more than five hundred venues in the United States and abroad. www.margepiercy.com.

A note on the type

The text of this book was set in Century, a type designed
in 1894 by Linn Boyd Benton (1844–1932). Benton cut
Century in response to a request by Theodore Low
De Vinne for an attractive, easy-to-read typeface to fit
the narrow columns of his *Century Magazine*. Early in
the 1900s Benton's son, Morris Fuller Benton (1872–
1948), working for his father's American Type Founders
Company, updated and improved Century in several
versions, such as Century Expanded, Century Old Style,
and Century Schoolbook. Century is the only American
typeface cut before 1910 that is still widely in use today.

Printed in the United States
by Baker & Taylor Publisher Services